TUNDRA
FOOD WEBS

WRITTEN BY PAUL FLEISHER
PHOTOGRAPHS BY GARY SCHULTZ

LERNER PUBLICATIONS COMPANY • MINNEAPOLIS

Additional photographs in this book are used with the permission of:
© BIOS/Peter Arnold, Inc., p. 13; © Scott T. Smith/CORBIS, p. 23; © Wiede, U. & M./Peter Arnold, Inc., p. 30; © Prisma/SuperStock, p. 33; © Joe McDonald/Visuals Unlimited, p. 37. Illustrations on pp. 4, 16 by Zeke Smith, © Lerner Publishing Group, Inc.; map on p. 10 © Laura Westlund/Independent Picture Service.

Text copyright © 2008 by Lerner Publishing Group, Inc.
Photographs copyright © 2008 by Gary Schultz, except where noted

Early Bird Food Webs series diagrams created by Zeke Smith.

Lerner Publications Company
A division of Lerner Publishing Group, Inc.
241 First Avenue North
Minneapolis, MN 55401 U.S.A.

Website address: www.lernerbooks.com

Library of Congress Cataloging-in-Publication Data

Fleisher, Paul.
    Tundra food webs / by Paul Fleisher.
      p.   cm. — (Early bird food webs)
    ISBN 978–0–8225–6727–1 (lib. bdg. : alk. paper)
    1. Tundra ecology—Juvenile literature. 2. Food chains (Ecology)—Juvenile literature. I. Title.
    QH541.5.T8F54 2008
    577.5'86—dc22   2006035850

Manufactured in the United States of America
1 2 3 4 5 6 – JR – 13 12 11 10 09 08

CONTENTS

A Tundra Food Web

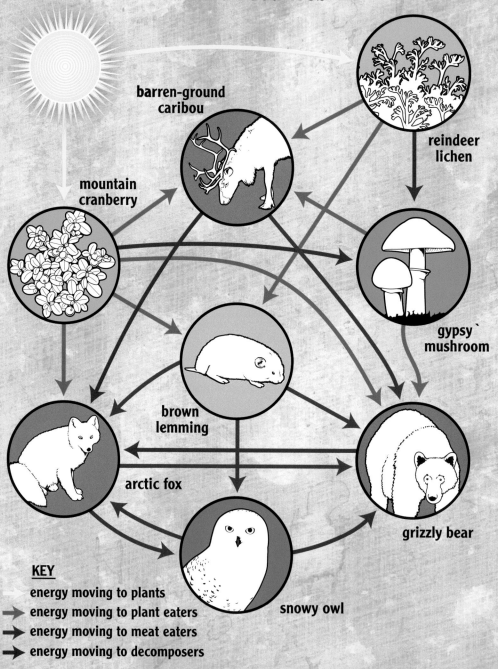

barren-ground
caribou

reindeer
lichen

mountain
cranberry

gypsy
mushroom

brown
lemming

arctic fox

grizzly bear

snowy owl

KEY
→ energy moving to plants
→ energy moving to plant eaters
→ energy moving to meat eaters
→ energy moving to decomposers

BE A WORD DETECTIVE

Can you find these words as you read about tundra food webs? Be a detective and try to figure out what they mean. You can turn to the glossary on page 46 for help.

active layer
bacteria
carnivores
consumers
decay

decomposers
environment
food chain
food web
herbivores

nutrients
omnivores
permafrost
photosynthesis
producers

The sun sets over the tundra in the winter. What is the tundra like during the winter?

The sun sets over the tundra in the winter. What is the tundra like during the winter?

CHAPTER 1
THE TUNDRA

The land of the far north is called the tundra.
It is a harsh place to live. Most of the tundra is
flat. No trees grow there. The air is dry.
Strong winds blow.

Winters are long and cold in the tundra.
The ground is frozen. It is covered with snow.
Some days, the sun never rises.

Tundra summers are short. They last only a couple of months. During the summer, the sun shines brightly. On some days, the sun never sets.

Each summer, the tundra buzzes with life. Flowers bloom. Birds raise their young. Insects fill the air.

Colorful wildflowers bloom in a tundra meadow.

Melting snow and ice form pools of water on the tundra. Some of the water drains into a nearby river.

In the summer, the top layer of soil thaws. That part of the ground is called the active layer. Plants and animals can live in the active layer.

Below the active layer, the ground stays frozen. The frozen layer is called permafrost. Permafrost is very deep.

In the summer, the snow melts. Water seeps into the active layer. But water cannot soak into the permafrost. The water has no place to go. So the surface of the tundra stays wet. Marshes and ponds form.

Each winter, the water freezes again. When water freezes, it expands. Ice pushes in all directions. Ice pushes up round hills called pingos. The ice also forms cracks across the land. From above, the tundra looks like a jigsaw puzzle.

A pingo forms when water freezes underground. When ice pushes up on the land, a hill forms.

The tundra is an important environment. An environment is the place where any creature lives. The environment includes the air, soil, and weather. It includes other plants and animals too.

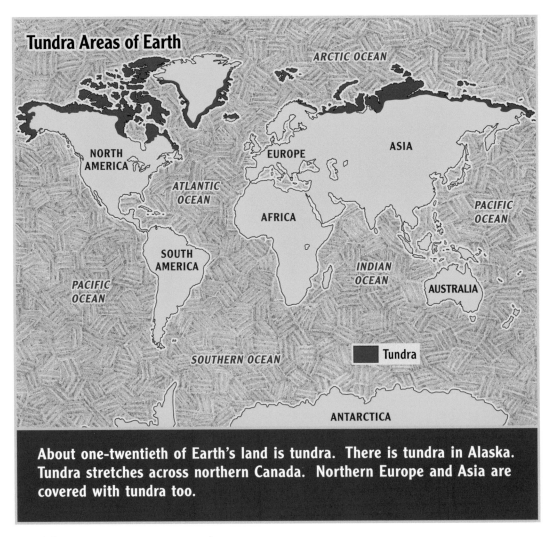

Tundra Areas of Earth

ARCTIC OCEAN

NORTH AMERICA

EUROPE

ASIA

ATLANTIC OCEAN

PACIFIC OCEAN

AFRICA

SOUTH AMERICA

INDIAN OCEAN

AUSTRALIA

PACIFIC OCEAN

SOUTHERN OCEAN

Tundra

ANTARCTICA

About one-twentieth of Earth's land is tundra. There is tundra in Alaska. Tundra stretches across northern Canada. Northern Europe and Asia are covered with tundra too.

Antlers and other animal bones slowly break down. They become part of the tundra's soil. New plants grow in the soil.

Living things on the tundra depend on one another. Some animals eat plants. Many animals eat other animals. Some creatures feed on plants and animals that have died. When plants and animals die, they break down into chemicals (KEH-muh-kuhlz). The chemicals become part of the soil. Some of these chemicals help plants grow.

The sun shines on a moose as he eats a willow plant. The moose gets some of the sun's energy from the willow.

Energy moves from one living thing to another. A food chain shows how living things get energy. Energy for life comes from the sun. Plants store the sun's energy in their leaves, stems, and roots. Animals eat the plants. They get some of the sun's energy from the plants. The energy moves along the food chain. When one creature eats another, some of the energy is passed on.

The tundra has many food chains. Here is one example. A willow plant gets energy from the sun. A lemming eats the leaves and stems of the willow. Then a fox eats the lemming. Later the fox dies. Tiny living things called bacteria (bak-TEER-ee-uh) feed on its body. The sun's energy goes from the plant to the lemming. Then some of the energy goes to the fox. Then some of it goes to the bacteria.

A collared lemming carries part of a dwarf willow through a tunnel in the active layer.

Lemmings do not eat only willow plants. They also eat lichens (LYE-kenz) and berries. Foxes eat other things besides lemmings. Foxes eat birds, eggs, and berries. Bacteria feed on all kinds of dead animals and plants. The tundra's many food chains make up a food web. A food web shows how all living things in an environment depend on one another for food.

An artic fox pounces on a small animal moving under the snow.

The tundra's energy comes from the sun. Northern primrose and other tundra plants use sunlight to make food. What else do plants make?

CHAPTER 2
TUNDRA PLANTS

Green plants use sunlight to make food. Living things that make their own food from sunlight are called producers. Plants also make oxygen (AHK-sih-juhn). Oxygen is a gas in the air. All animals need oxygen to breathe.

15

Plants make food and oxygen through photosynthesis (FOH-toh-SIHN-thuh-sihs). Plants need carbon dioxide, sunlight, and water for photosynthesis. Carbon dioxide is a gas in the air. Plant leaves take in carbon dioxide and sunlight. The roots take in water. Plants use energy from the sunlight to turn the carbon dioxide and water into sugar and starch. Sugar and starch are the plant's own food. Plants store this food in their leaves and roots.

Photosynthesis

sunlight

carbon dioxide

oxygen

water (from roots)

Cotton grass turns sunlight, carbon dioxide, and water into food for itself.

An arctic ground squirrel sniffs a tundra flower.

When plants make food, they also make oxygen. The oxygen goes into the air. Animals breathe the oxygen. They breathe out carbon dioxide. Plants use the carbon dioxide to make more food.

The roots of tundra plants take in water from the active layer. The water comes from melted ice and snow.

Plants grow in soil. The soil contains chemicals called nutrients (NOO-tree-uhnts). Living things need nutrients to grow. Water soaks into the soil. Nutrients from the soil go into the water. The plants' roots take in the water and get nutrients from the soil. The nutrients become part of each plant.

On the tundra, there is little sunshine in the winter. Snow falls and stays on the ground. But plants live under the snow. They have stored the food they made in the summer. Animals depend on the energy stored in those plants.

An arctic ground squirrel eats seeds from grass that is covered by snow.

Crowberry, bearberry, and cranberry plants grow fruit that animals eat.

Tundra plants grow for only about two months each year. Their roots can grow only in the active layer. Plants cannot send roots into the permafrost. So the plants grow in the summer, when the active layer is unfrozen.

In the summer, the tundra is covered with colorful plants. Flowers bloom. Many tundra plants have berries. Cranberries and blueberries make good food for animals.

Sedges also grow on the tundra. Sedges look like grass. Cotton grass is a sedge that grows in thick clumps. It grows in drier parts of the tundra. Sedges also grow in wet areas. Moss grows in the marshes too.

Reindeer lichen grows on the tundra all year. Lichens are algae (AL-jee) and fungi (FUHN-jye) growing together. Animals eat lichens in the winter.

Lichens are plantlike living things. Reindeer lichens are important producers on the tundra.

A caribou eats plants during a snowfall. What other tundra animals eat plants?

CHAPTER 3
TUNDRA PLANT EATERS

Living things that eat other living things are consumers. *Consume* means "eat." Animals are consumers.

Animals that eat plants are called herbivores (ER-buh-vorz). The sun's energy is stored in the plants. When an animal eats a plant, it gets the sun's energy.

Many tundra insects feed on plants.
During the summer, insects eat leaves and roots.
Bumblebees fly from flower to flower. They
drink from the flowers. Other insects live in
ponds. They eat plants growing in the water.

A bumblebee rests on the flower of a fireweed.

Many birds migrate to the tundra each summer. They travel there to find plants to eat. Millions of geese fly to the tundra. Swans and ducks go there too. They eat pond plants and grasses. They make nests and raise their young.

Two geese find grasses to eat in a tundra pond.

Rock ptarmigans have white feathers in the winter and brown feathers in the summer.

Ptarmigans (TAHR-mih-guhnz) live on the tundra all year. These birds are much like chickens. In the winter, ptarmigans scratch away snow to find food. They eat seeds and berries. Ptarmigans grow white feathers each winter. The white color helps them hide in the snow. They hide from other tundra animals.

The fur of some tundra mammals turns white in the winter. Arctic hares are white. In the summer, some arctic hares grow brown fur.

Lemmings stay busy all year. They tunnel under the snow. They search for seeds and berries. They eat plant stems and roots. Voles look like mice. Voles tunnel under the snow all winter too. They search for plants to eat.

An arctic hare nibbles on a plant in the winter. Artic hares eat the leaves and stems of tundra plants.

Musk oxen's thick hair helps them stay warm during tundra winters.

Musk oxen are the largest herbivores on the tundra. They live there all year. Musk oxen kick snow away with their hooves. They eat the plants underneath the snow.

In the summer, moose, elk, and caribou (KEHR-uh-boo) come to feed on tundra plants. Caribou travel in large herds. They eat willows and sedges in the summer. Each winter, most caribou travel south. They migrate to find more food. A few stay on the tundra all winter. They eat lichens.

A Lapland longspur has caught a juicy caterpillar to eat. What are animals that eat other animals called?

CHAPTER 4
TUNDRA
MEAT EATERS

Carnivores (KAHR-nuh-vorz) are animals that eat meat. They catch and eat other animals. But carnivores depend on plants too.

Carnivores get energy from eating animals that

Many biting insects live in the tundra. Mosquitoes are carnivores. They feed on the blood of birds and mammals. Gnats and flies also feed on blood.

Fish swim in the rivers and lakes. A kind of fish called arctic char eats insects. It also eats other small animals. So do grayling and whitefish.

Mosquitoes are feeding on the blood of this loon.

This snowy owl caught a lemming for its next meal.

Some tundra birds are carnivores. Snowy owls hunt lemmings and voles. In the summer, millions of other birds migrate to the tundra to find animals to eat. Baby birds feast on insects. Falcons and cranes hunt for other birds. Cranes also eat fish and small mammals. So do eagles.

Wolves catch many animals in the summertime. Wolves travel in packs. They hunt small mammals and birds. Wolves kill and eat caribou too.

A wolf eats an animal that it killed.

Some animals eat both plants and animals. These animals are called omnivores (AHM-nuh-vorz). Arctic foxes are omnivores. Foxes eat many different things. They catch lemmings and voles. They also eat birds and eggs. But foxes eat berries too.

Grizzly bears are omnivores. They eat small mammals. They hunt caribou and catch fish. Grizzly bears also eat fruit and berries.

Grizzly bears migrate to the tundra in the summer to find food. This grizzly bear found some blueberries to eat.

The bones of a dead fish lie on the shore. What living things feed on dead animals?

CHAPTER 5

TUNDRA DECOMPOSERS

All living things die. When plants or animals die, they decay. They break down into nutrients. Living things called decomposers help dead things decay. Decomposers feed on dead creatures.

Tiny decomposers are feeding on the body of this caribou. They are breaking it down into nutrients.

Decomposers are nature's recyclers. They break down dead plants and animals. Nutrients from the dead things go back into the soil. Other living things can use those nutrients to grow. Without decomposers, dead plants and animals would cover the tundra. Then no new plants could grow. Animals would run out of food.

Dead creatures decay slowly on the tundra. For most of the year, everything is frozen. It is too cold for things to decay. Nutrients do not go back into the soil quickly. So tundra soil has few nutrients. That is another reason why tundra plants grow slowly.

Decomposers will feed slowly on these remains of a musk ox. It could take many years for them to break down the body.

Some tundra animals are scavengers. They find and eat the meat of dead animals. Ravens are scavengers. These birds look for animals that have died. Foxes follow large carnivores. The large carnivores hunt and kill other animals to eat. Later, foxes eat what is left.

A grizzly bear digs up the body of a moose that it killed and buried. Two ravens wait to sneak a bite of what is left.

This pile of droppings contains berries and other food that a bear ate. Young flies and beetles will feed on the droppings.

Worms feed on dead plants and animals. They help the dead creatures rot away. So do insects such as beetles and flies. Some insects feed on droppings from animals.

Mushrooms and other fungi are decomposers. They grow during the wet summer season. They feed on dead plants.

Bacteria are the most important decomposers. They are so tiny we cannot see them. Bacteria feed on all kinds of dead plants and animals.

A mushroom grows among bearberry shrubs.

This man is ice fishing near an island village in Alaska. Do many people live on the tundra?

CHAPTER 6

PEOPLE AND THE TUNDRA

Few people live on the tundra. It is too cold.

There are no large cities. There are no farms.

But some people do live on the tundra.

Some native people live by hunting and fishing.

Others have moved to towns.

In Europe and Asia, some people herd reindeer. Reindeer are a kind of caribou. People living on the tundra eat reindeer meat. They make clothing from reindeer skin.

Some people work on the tundra. They hunt. They also trap animals for fur. But they have to be careful not to kill too many animals.

Years ago, hunters killed almost all the musk oxen in North America. People had to stop hunting them. More musk oxen live in Canada and Alaska again.

A huge machine drills for oil deep beneath the surface near Prudhoe Bay, Alaska.

Some parts of the tundra have valuable metals under the ground. There is also oil deep underground. People work in mines to get metals. Others work on oil wells.

People must be careful when they mine or drill in the tundra. Oil drilling uses heavy machines. So does mining. The machines can damage the tundra. And oil spills kill plants and animals. Tundra plants grow slowly. If they are damaged, the plants take many years to grow back.

The Trans-Alaska pipeline carries oil across Alaska. The pipes were built above the ground on the tundra. That way, the oil does not melt the permafrost.

Polar bears live only in the far north. They hunt animals that live in or near the Arctic Ocean. But warm temperatures are melting the ice where they hunt.

The greatest danger to the tundra is Earth's changing climate. The world is slowly getting warmer. More tundra ice melts each year. Tundra plants and animals need the cold to live. As the tundra gets warmer, they may die out or move away. Other creatures may take their place.

The tundra is a very special place. Many creatures that live there live nowhere else. We must take care of the tundra.

ON SHARING A BOOK

When you share a book with a child, you show that reading is important. To get the most out of the experience, read in a comfortable, quiet place. Turn off the television and limit other distractions, such as telephone calls. Be prepared to start slowly. Take turns reading parts of this book. Stop occasionally and discuss what you're reading. Talk about the photographs. If the child begins to lose interest, stop reading. When you pick up the book again, revisit the parts you have already read.

BE A VOCABULARY DETECTIVE

The word list on page 5 contains words that are important in understanding the topic of this book. Be word detectives and search for the words as you read the book together. Talk about what the words mean and how they are used in the sentence. Do any of these words have more than one meaning? You will find the words defined in a glossary on page 46.

WHAT ABOUT QUESTIONS?

Use questions to make sure the child understands the information in this book. Here are some suggestions:

> What did this paragraph tell us? What does this picture show? What is a food web? How do plants depend on animals? Where does energy in the tundra come from? What do we call animals that eat both plants and animals? How can oil drilling hurt tundra animals? What is your favorite part of the book? Why?

If the child has questions, don't hesitate to respond with questions of your own, such as: What do *you* think? Why? What is it that you don't know? If the child can't remember certain facts, turn to the index.

INTRODUCING THE INDEX

The index helps readers find information without searching through the whole book. Turn to the index on page 48. Choose an entry such as *plants* and ask the child to use the index to find out how plants make their own food. Repeat with as many entries as you like. Ask the child to point out the differences between an index and a glossary. (The index helps readers find information, while the glossary tells readers what words mean.)

THE TUNDRA AND FOOD WEBS

BOOKS

Capeci, Anne. *Food Chain Frenzy.* New York: Scholastic, 2003. Take a ride on the Magic School Bus with Ms. Frizzle and her class as they explore photosynthesis, food chains, and food webs.

Hiscock, Bruce. *The Big Caribou Herd: Life in the Arctic National Wildlife Refuge.* Honesdale, PA: Boyds Mill Press, 2003. Follow a herd of caribou migrating across tundra lands.

Johnson, Rebecca L. *A Walk in the Tundra.* Minneapolis: Carolrhoda Books, 2001. See plants and animals that live on the North American tundra.

Markle, Sandra. *Wolves.* Minneapolis: Lerner Publications Company, 2004. Go on a hunt with wolves, carnivores of the tundra.

Squire, Ann O. *Lemmings.* New York: Children's Press, 2007. Learn more about the life cycle of these tundra herbivores.

WEBSITES

Biomes of the World—Tundra
http://www.mbgnet.net/sets/tundra
Follow Michael and Ashley on their journey around the North Pole.

Chain Reaction
http://www.ecokids.ca/pub/eco_info/topics/frogs/chain_reaction/
Create a food chain and find out what happens if one link is taken out of the chain.

Tundra Animal Printouts—EnchantedLearning.com
http://www.enchantedlearning.com/biomes/tundra/tundra.shtml
Click on a tundra animal to learn what it looks like and what it eats.

GLOSSARY

active layer: the top layer of tundra soil that thaws each summer. Plants and animals live in this layer.

bacteria (bak-TEER-ee-uh): tiny living things made of just one cell. Bacteria can be seen only under a microscope.

carnivores (KAHR-nuh-vorz): animals that eat meat

consumers: living things that eat other living things. Animals are consumers.

decay: to break down

decomposers: living things that feed on dead plants and animals and break them down into nutrients

environment: a place where a creature lives. An environment includes the air, soil, weather, plants, and animals in a place.

food chain: the way energy moves from the sun to a plant, then to a plant eater, then to a meat eater, and finally to a decomposer

food web: many food chains connected together. A food web shows how all living things in a place need each other for food.

herbivores (ER-buh-vorz): animals that eat plants

lichens (LYE-kenz): plantlike living things that are part algae and part fungi

mammals: animals that feed their babies milk and have hair on their bodies

nutrients (NOO-tree-uhnts): chemicals that living things need in order to grow

omnivores (AHM-nuh-vorz): animals that eat both plants and animals

permafrost: the layer of soil under the tundra that stays frozen all year

photosynthesis (FOH-toh-SIHN-thuh-sihs): the way green plants use energy from sunlight to make their own food from carbon dioxide and water

producers: living things that make their own food. Plants are producers.

INDEX

Pages listed in **bold** type refer to photographs.